T0014422

CRICKETS
at Night

Kathleen A. Klatte

PowerKiDS press™
New York

Published in 2021 by The Rosen Publishing Group, Inc.
29 East 21st Street, New York, NY 10010

Copyright © 2021 by The Rosen Publishing Group, Inc.

All rights reserved. No part of this book may be reproduced in any form without permission in writing from the publisher, except by a reviewer.

Portions of this work were originally authored by Doreen Gonzales and published as *Crickets at Night*. All new material this edition authored by Kathleen A. Klatte.

Editor: Kathleen Klatte
Book Design: Michael Flynn

Photo Credits: Cover Angel Simon/Shutterstock.com; (series background) MoreThanPicture/Shutterstock.com; p. 4 PetrP/Shutterstock.com; p. 5 Elliotte Rusty Harold/Shutterstock.com; p. 6 witoon/Shutterstock.com; p. 7 encikAn/Shutterstock.com; p. 9 Andaman/Shutterstock.com; p. 11 Bildagentur Zoonar GmbH/Shutterstock.com; p. 12 MF Photo/Shutterstock.com; p. 13 Ramlan Bin Abdul Jalil/Shutterstock.com; p. 15 MadeK/Shutterstock.com; p. 16 D. Kucharski/Shutterstock.com; p. 17 GoWithLight/Shutterstock.com; p. 18 japa1991/Shutterstock.com; p. 19 Ciliegia10S/Shutterstock.com; p. 21 Jon Arnold/AWL Images/Getty Images; p. 22 ilikestudio/Shutterstock.com.

Library of Congress Cataloging-in-Publication Data

Names: Klatte, Kathleen A., author.
Title: Crickets at night / Kathleen A. Klatte.
Description: New York : PowerKids Press, [2021] | Series: Up all night!
   nocturnal animals | Includes index.
Identifiers: LCCN 2019047634 | ISBN 9781725318694 (paperback) | ISBN
   9781725318717 (library binding) | ISBN 9781725318700 (6 pack)
Subjects: LCSH: Crickets–Juvenile literature. | Nocturnal
   animals–Juvenile literature.
Classification: LCC QL508.G8 K585 2021 | DDC 595.7/26–dc23
LC record available at https://lccn.loc.gov/2019047634

Some of the images in this book illustrate individuals who are models. The depictions do not imply actual situations or events.

Manufactured in the United States of America

CPSIA Compliance Information: Batch #CSPK20. For Further Information contact Rosen Publishing, New York, New York at 1-800-237-9932.

CONTENTS

HERE, THERE, AND EVERYWHERE

One of the most familiar sounds of a summer night is crickets chirping. Most crickets are **nocturnal**. These **insects** spend their days sleeping in the grass and under logs. At night, they come out to eat and sing. A few kinds of crickets are **crepuscular**. They begin their songs as the sun sets.

There are thousands of kinds of crickets. The largest are about 2 inches (5.1 cm) long. The littlest crickets are smaller than many ants. Crickets live almost everywhere in the world. You can find them in all sorts of **habitats**.

YOU NEED TO BE VERY CAREFUL AND QUIET TO SPOT A CRICKET. THEIR COLORING BLENDS INTO THEIR HABITAT. THIS CRICKET IS THE SAME COLOR AS THE TREE IT LIVES ON.

5

LOTS OF LEGS

Crickets are generally black, brown, or green. These dark colors hide crickets from nighttime predators. Some crickets are gray or light green. This makes them hard to see against the rocks or leaves where they hide during the day.

Crickets have six legs. The insects' four front legs are shorter than the two in back. A cricket's ears are on its two front legs!

A CRICKET'S HIND LEGS ARE MUCH LARGER AND STRONGER THAN ITS FRONT LEGS. CRICKETS' FEET ARE **SEGMENTED** TO HELP THEM JUMP.

Crickets have two long antennae coming from their head. These antennae are often longer than the cricket's body! Crickets use antennae to feel and smell what's around them. This can be more useful than eyesight at night.

WHILE YOU'RE SLEEPING

Crickets, grasshoppers, and locusts all belong to the scientific order Orthoptera. They are all leaping insects with strong hind legs. Katydids are crickets' closest relatives.

A SKELETON ON THE OUTSIDE

A cricket wears its skeleton on the outside of its body. This skeleton is called an exoskeleton. It holds a cricket's soft body parts and keeps them from getting hurt. Cricket bodies have three parts: a head, a **thorax**, and an **abdomen**.

Crickets outgrow their exoskeletons many times. Each time a cricket gets too big for its shell, the exoskeleton breaks open. The cricket crawls out of its shell and a new, larger exoskeleton grows around the cricket. Shedding the shell is called molting. A cricket grows a little bigger each time it molts. A cricket stops molting when it's fully grown.

THIS CRICKET IS MOLTING. IT'S CRAWLING AWAY FROM ITS OLD EXOSKELETON. YOU CAN SEE HOW MUCH BIGGER THE CRICKET IS NOW.

9

SO MANY CRICKETS!

Scientists recognize more than 2,000 species, or kinds, of crickets. Field crickets are common. They live in fields, yards, and buildings. These black or brown crickets are about 1.2 inches (31 mm) long. House crickets also live in many places. They like to live in buildings where they can stay warm.

Mole crickets dig underground tunnels. Three species aren't native to the United States, and they're considered pests because they **damage** crops.

Tree crickets live in trees and bushes. The snowy tree cricket's song is used often in film and TV backgrounds. There are ways people can figure out the temperature by counting the cricket's chirps.

THIS IS A MOLE CRICKET. IT'S NOT A MEMBER OF THE CRICKET FAMILY GRYLLIDAE, ALTHOUGH IT'S STILL CALLED A CRICKET. ITS FORELEGS ARE MADE FOR DIGGING.

WHILE YOU'RE SLEEPING

Until the middle of the 20th century, scientists thought all field crickets in the United States belonged to the same species. People studied their songs to figure out how many different species there really are.

11

JUMPING BUGS

Most crickets don't use their two sets of wings to fly. Some can't fly at all. Instead, they use their wings to help them jump. Crickets use their powerful hind legs to jump away from danger. Nocturnal predators often lose sight of crickets after they jump into the darkness.

CRICKETS HAVE THREE SETS OF LEGS. THE TWO SMALLER SETS ARE CALLED WALKING LEGS. THE MUCH LARGER HIND LEGS ARE CALLED JUMPING LEGS.

Many common types of crickets can jump about 3 feet (0.9 m) at once. This can be about 30 times their body length. Jumping is a cricket's best defense, along with keeping silent when it senses another animal approaching. If a cricket can't escape, it can use its legs to fight.

MUSIC OF THE NIGHT

You're probably familiar with the sound of crickets chirping. However, only male crickets chirp. They do this to call females to them or to tell other male crickets to go away.

Crickets chirp by moving one wing over the other. One forewing has a scraper that moves along a row of teeth on the opposite forewing. These teeth look a little like a comb.

Different crickets have different types of songs. Some crickets chirp only at night. Other crickets chirp during the day and night. Crickets chirp more as the temperature rises. This means you'll hear crickets in late spring and throughout summer.

WHILE YOU'RE SLEEPING

Cricket song isn't just pleasant to listen to, it's a sign of a healthy **environment**. Each type of living thing—insect, plant, or animal—plays an important part in the food web.

IF YOU WALK TOWARD A CRICKET, IT'LL STOP CHIRPING. CRICKETS SENSE NOISES AND **VIBRATIONS** AND WILL STOP CHIRPING IN CASE A PREDATOR IS NEARBY.

15

IT ALL STARTS WITH AN EGG

Like many other types of insects, crickets start out as eggs. Some types of crickets lay their eggs in soil. Other kinds lay eggs in tree bark or on plant leaves or stems. Female crickets of many kinds lay their eggs just before the coldest part of the year. The eggs stay there until the weather warms and baby crickets hatch from them.

A FEMALE CRICKET LAID THESE EGGS IN THE SOIL. WHEN FEMALE CRICKETS LAY THEIR EGGS IN OR ON PLANTS, IT MAY DAMAGE THE PLANTS.

Baby crickets are called nymphs. Nymphs look very much like adult crickets. Nymphs often molt eight to 10 times before they are fully grown. Adult crickets live for six to eight weeks. They die as the temperatures drop.

WHAT'S FOR DINNER?

Crickets eat all sorts of things. They eat grass, leaves, seeds, and smaller insects. Crickets sometimes also eat dead animals and even other crickets. Crickets that live indoors will feed on cloth, leather, and paper.

Their nocturnal ways keep crickets safe from some daytime predators. However, many nighttime predators, such as birds, spiders, skunks, raccoons, and foxes, eat crickets.

In many places, people eat crickets and other types of insects. Chocolate-covered crickets are popular in some places. In Thailand and Mexico, cooked crickets are often sold by street vendors as snacks.

IN MANY PARTS OF THE WORLD, IT'S COMMON TO SEE INSECTS SOLD BY STREET FOOD VENDORS. SOMETIMES THEY'RE EVEN SOLD IN RESTAURANTS AND FOOD SHOPS.

WHILE YOU'RE SLEEPING

Companies are looking into cricket farming as a good source of **protein** for people. Some people think it could be a **sustainable** source of food for the world's growing population.

LIFE WITH CRICKETS

People interact with crickets in many ways. In some places, they're considered lucky. Some people keep male crickets because they like to hear the crickets' chirping. They put the crickets in cages so they can listen to their nighttime songs.

People also use crickets as pet food. They feed them to their frogs, turtles, and lizards.

In some parts of the world, people enjoy watching crickets fight. When they want to watch a fight, the people put two crickets together and make them angry. A cricket fight lasts only a few seconds. The fight ends when one of the crickets stops chirping or tries to get away.

WHILE YOU'RE SLEEPING

There are many species of crickets that are native to North America. There are also crickets that arrived hidden in cargo from other countries. These are called invasive species, and they can crowd out the species that are native to an area.

CHINESE PEOPLE HAVE KEPT CRICKETS AS PETS FOR CENTURIES. IT'S VERY COMMON TO SEE THEM FOR SALE IN MARKETPLACES.

21

SHARING THE WORLD WITH CRICKETS

Some people think that crickets are pests that need to be controlled or destroyed. These insects sometimes find their way into homes and eat food or damage things. Outside, large numbers of crickets can destroy crops and other plants.

However, crickets are an important part of nature. Many birds and animals need crickets for food. Crickets also help keep Earth's soil healthy. The insects' bodies break up the plants they eat and produce droppings, which go into the soil and make it rich. This makes plants grow better. Crickets are not only useful, but they also make our lives better. Can you imagine a summer evening without crickets singing?

GLOSSARY

abdomen: The rear part of an insect's body.

crepuscular: Occurring or active during twilight.

damage: To do harm to something.

environment: The natural world.

habitat: The natural home for plants, animals, and other living things.

insect: A small animal that has six legs and a body formed of three parts and that may have wings.

nocturnal: Active mainly during the night.

protein: A substance found in foods (such as meat, milk, eggs, and beans) that is an important part of the human diet.

segmented: Made of segments, or sections.

sustainable: Able to last a long time.

thorax: The middle section of an insect's body.

vibration: Small, quick movements.

INDEX

WEBSITES

Due to the changing nature of Internet links, PowerKids Press has developed an online list of websites related to the subject of this book. This site is updated regularly. Please use this link to access the list: www.powerkidslinks.com/uan/crickets